FRIENDLY FOOD

FROM BREAKFAST TO DESSERT

FRIENDLY FOOD
All Rights Reserved
Copyright © BOKFÖRLAGET MAX STRÖM

Original title: *FRIENDLY FOOD – MAT UTAN GLUTEN, SOCKER OCH MJÖLK*
ISBN 978-91-7126-312-4

Text, design and photography: Hanna Göransson
Editing and proofing: Elisabet Sahlin
Recipe checking: Kristina Valentin
Repro: Italgraf Media, Stockholm

Disclaimer
The information and recipes printed in this book are provided to the best of our knowledge and belief and from our own experience. However neither the author nor the publisher shall accept liability for any damage whatsoever which may arise directly or indirectly from the use of this book. It is advisable not to serve dishes that contain raw eggs to very young children, pregnant women, elderly people, or to anyone weakened by serious illness. If in any doubt, consult your doctor. Be sure that all the eggs you use are as fresh as possible. Please note that bee pollen can be dangerous to those with allergies to bees, their products or other seasonal allergies.

© for this English edition: h.f.ullmann publishing GmbH

Translation from Swedish: JMS Books llp in association with Malcolm Garrard
Typesetting: cbdesign
Cover photos: Hanna Göransson

Overall responsibility for production: h.f.ullmann publishing GmbH, Potsdam, Germany

Printed in Poland, 2015

ISBN 978-3-8480-0871-1

10 9 8 7 6 5 4 3 2 1
X IX VIII VII VI V IV III II I

www.ullmann-publishing.com
newsletter@ullmann-publishing.com
facebook.com/ullmann.social

MIX
Papier aus verantwor-
tungsvollen Quellen
FSC
www.fsc.org
FSC® C015559

Abbreviations and Quantities
1 oz = 1 ounce = 28 grams
1 lb = 1 pound = 16 ounces 1
1 cup = approx. 5–8 ounces* (see below)
1 cup = 8 fluid ounces = 250 milliliters (liquids)
2 cups = 1 pint (liquids) = 15 milliliters (liquids)
8 pints = 4 quarts = 1 gallon (liquids)
1 g = 1 gram = 1/1000 kilogram = 5 ml (liquids)
1 kg = 1 kilogram = 1000 grams = 2¼ lb
1 l = 1 liter = 1000 milliliters (ml) = 1 quart
125 milliliters (ml) = approx. 8 tablespoons = ½ cup
1 tbsp = 1 level tablespoon = 15–20 g* (depending on density) = 15 milliliters (liquids)
1 tsp = 1 level teaspoon = 3–5 g * (depending on density) = 5 ml (liquids)

*The weight of dry ingredients varies significantly depending on the density factor, e.g. 1 cup of flour weighs less than 1 cup of butter. Quantities in ingredients have been rounded up or down for convenience, where appropriate. Metric conversions may therefore not correspond exactly. It is important to use either American or metric measurements within a recipe.
The purpose of the recipes and advice in this book is simply to give guidance on quality nutrition and how to increase your energy. If you have a medical condition you should consult your doctor.

FRIENDLY FOOD

FROM BREAKFAST TO DESSERT

GLUTEN-FREE, DAIRY-FREE,
AND WITHOUT ADDED SUGAR

HANNA GÖRANSSON

h.f.ullmann

CONTENTS

FOREWORD

....

I'm thrilled that you are reading this book. Its 160 beautiful pages feature recipes that are fun, simple, and packed with both joy and love. I very much enjoy sharing the things I consider to be good for me: excellent food that fuels the body with high-quality energy, exercise, and a mind full of lovely thoughts, lively laughter, and creativity. Do you long for a body that is in proper balance? Good—you've already taken a step in the right direction. I believe that every individual needs to find their own way to well-being: discovering the right path and the best fuel for your own body is an exciting journey that will continue throughout your life. Both body and mind change with time. Your body is the most beautiful thing you have, so give it what it wants and what it needs.

A few years ago I started to thoroughly enjoy exercise. It became an intrinsic part of my life, as did taking control of what I was eating every day. The training put me in touch with how my body actually felt and I began to take an interest in the important role played by food. A drastic reduction in my intake of gluten, refined sugar, simple carbohydrates, and most dairy products led to a fitter, stronger, and happier me. Once you find the right thing for you, it becomes both easy and fun. I had never imagined that cutting out a few ingredients and adding a few new ones would make that much difference to my well-being, but it suddenly opened up a whole new world of exciting foodstuffs and new ways to bake and cook.

I am neither Sweden's next health guru nor a celebrity chef, but I hope to inspire you to take a step in the right direction, with no harsh rules to obey or difficult hoops to jump through. I want your health to make you happy and to become a natural part of your daily life. Make it your goal to have a body that is in balance by living life to the full, both physically and mentally. This book is all about simple ways of making delicious food that is a treat for the eyes and the taste buds.

Here are a few of my favorite recipes.

Hanna Göransson

P.S. If you want to follow my Swedish-language blog, you'll find me at this address: hurbrasomhelst.se

TIPS & TECHNIQUES

Coconut milk & coconut cream

Coconut milk is liquid and creamy. If you shake the container slightly, it should make a lapping sound. Coconut milk is always good to use in smoothies, soups, baked goods, and casseroles. I always use the full-fat version.

Coconut cream has a firmer texture. When shaken in its packaging, it will sound more solid. You can buy it in its solid form or with a firm top section and coconut water below; it is very important that you use only the solid part for recipes that call for coconut cream.

Whisking coconut cream

Separate the solid and liquid parts and use an electric mixer to whisk the solid cream until it is fluffy. You could also stir in some real vanilla powder and a dash of lemon juice at the end. The photograph opposite shows how the water has been reserved in a jar and the solid portion whipped into a cream. Save the liquid, which is really delicious when used in smoothies, in baking, or as a sauce base. I always use full-fat coconut cream.

Tip You can also turn liquid coconut milk into cream by placing the container in the freezer for about two hours. This will separate the solid portion from the coconut water and you can then easily whip the solid part into a cream once it has thawed.

Instead of eggs

For those of you who don't eat eggs, these two options make delicious egg substitutes in breads, pancakes, cakes, and more.

1 flaxseed egg: Mix 2 tbsp/15 g ground flaxseeds with 3 tbsp/45 ml water and simmer in a saucepan until you have a jelly-like mass.

1 chia egg: Mix 4 tsp/15 g chia seeds with 3 tbsp/45 ml cold water until you have a jelly-like mass.

Sweeteners

In this book, I have chosen to use agave syrup, coconut sugar, fruit, and berries as sweeteners; yacon syrup, honey, and stevia are other good options.

Fine and coarse flour

Almond and coconut flour are available in both coarse and fine versions: the spoon in the photograph opposite shows fine grind (above) and coarse grind flour (below). Knowing the difference is important, as finely ground flour absorbs more liquid than the coarser alternative. Almond flour is more commonly found as coarse grind, as used in my recipes. Coconut flour is usually finely ground and this is the version I use.

Nut butters & nut milks

Nut butters are made by grinding nuts to a paste. In recipes where nut butter is listed as an ingredient, try different varieties according to your tastes—you might like to try hazelnut, almond, or peanut butter, for example. You'll find the basic recipe on page 79 but you can also buy it ready-made.

Nut milks are formed by nuts mixed with water and then strained as a smooth liquid. Varieties include almond, hazelnut, and sesame. You'll find the basic recipe on page 46. If a recipe says "any nut milk," use your favorite. They are also available ready-made.

Grocery and health food stores

You'll find most of the ingredients in this book in well-stocked grocery stores, and many are also available in health food stores or online.

Sticky batter

Baking without gluten, dairy, or sugar is different from traditional baking—think sticky batter rather than dough. The recipes tell you how the batter should look and give easy instructions to follow when shaping bread or rolling out pizza batter, for example.

Husk fiber

This is made from ground psyllium seeds and serves as a binding agent in baking and cooking.

Coconut oil

This is used extensively in my recipes and should be extra virgin and cold-pressed.

BREAKFAST
&
SNACKS

SCONES

baked with teff & quinoa flour

⅓ cup/50 g quinoa flour
⅓ cup/50 g light teff flour
⅓ cup/30 g ground flaxseeds
2 tsp/10 g psyllium husk
  fiber
2 tsp/10 g baking powder
Scant ¼ tsp/1.25 g herb salt
Scant 1 cup/225 ml any milk
2 tbsp/30 ml melted
  coconut oil
Seeds or nuts, for topping

Makes 4 scones.

Preheat the oven to 350°F/175°C.

Mix all the dry ingredients together in a bowl, then stir in the milk and the melted coconut oil. Let the batter stand and expand for 5 minutes.

Moisten your hands slightly and shape the mixture into 4 patties. Place the scones on a cookie sheet lined with baking parchment and sprinkle with seeds or nuts.

Bake in the oven for about 15 minutes, until risen and golden.

Tips You can use coarsely ground flours such as almond, chickpea, sesame, or buckwheat flour in the batter. A good rule of thumb is that the batter is ready when it has expanded and is tacky, but you can still easily shape it with moistened hands.

SUNFLOWER BREAD

with chia jam & coconut cream

1 cup/250 g sunflower seed
  butter (room temperature)
4 large eggs, separated
½ tbsp/7.5 ml agave syrup
7 tbsp/100 ml any milk
1 tbsp/15 ml cider vinegar
¼ cup/25 g coconut flour
1 tsp/5 g baking powder
½ tsp/2.5 g coarse salt

Makes 1 loaf.

Preheat the oven to 300°F/150°C and place an oven-proof bowl filled with water at the bottom of the oven; this will improve the color and crust of the bread. Line the base of a round, rectangular, or square loaf pan with baking parchment.

Mix the sunflower seed butter and egg yolks together in a mixer or with a hand blender, then add the agave syrup, milk, and vinegar. Beat the egg whites to stiff peaks. Mix the dry ingredients together in another bowl.

When the oven is up to heat, mix the dry ingredients into the batter. Fold ⅓ of the egg whites into the batter and mix gently. Now mix in the rest of the egg whites until you have a smooth, finely textured batter. Tip the batter into the pan and bake for about 50 minutes or until the bread is golden brown.

Let the bread cool in the pan for 15–20 minutes, then loosen the sides with a knife and turn it out on to a wire rack. Remove the baking parchment then turn the bread the right way up and let cool completely.

The bread will keep for up to a week in the refrigerator. It also freezes well.

Serve with chia jam and plain coconut cream (and see page 83 for chia jam recipes).

Tips

Coconut flour is rich in protein and fiber. It has a sweetish taste and is especially useful for adding fiber to your smoothie or porridge. Other butters you can use instead of sunflower seed include almond, hazelnut, cashew, flaxseed, hemp seed, or pumpkin seed butter. You'll find the recipe for nut butter on page 79.

BLUEBERRY BREAD

with grated zucchini (courgette)

1 cup/150 g buckwheat flour
Generous ¾ cup/100 g
    coarse almond flour
1 tbsp/15 g psyllium husk
    fiber
⅔ cup/65 g ground flaxseeds
1 tsp/5 g baking powder
1 tsp/5 g baking soda
Pinch of herb salt
4 inch/10 cm zucchini
    (courgette), grated
2 tbsp/30 ml melted
    coconut oil
2 eggs
Generous ¾ cup/200 ml
    any milk
¾ cup/70 g blueberries

Makes 1 loaf.

Preheat the oven to 390°F/200°C.

Combine all the dry ingredients in a bowl. Add remaining ingredients (except the blueberries) and mix well. The batter should be thick and stiff, but not dry. Dilute with more milk if necessary. Add the blueberries at the end.

Line an approx. 2½-pint/1½-liter loaf pan with baking parchment. Press down the batter, smoothing the surface, and bake the bread in the oven for 45–50 minutes. The bread will have a crispy crust. Let cool on a wire rack before slicing.

The bread will keep for about a week in the refrigerator and also freezes well.

Tips   You can use a different flour pretty much every time you make this bread—options include hazelnut, sesame, chickpea, teff, quinoa, amaranth, millet, and coconut flour. A good guideline to remember is that the batter should be thick and a little stiff, but not dry.

SEED CRISPBREAD

with egg, red cabbage, bell peppers & arugula

⅔ cup/100 g flour, e.g.
  quinoa or chickpea
7 tbsp/70 g sesame seeds
¼ cup/30 g sunflower seeds
⅓ cup/35 g pumpkin seeds
3 tbsp/30 g chia seeds
Scant ¼ tsp/1.25 g herb salt
1 cup/250 ml boiling water
1 tbsp/15 ml coconut oil

Makes 30–35 slices.

Preheat the oven to 350°F/175°C.

Combine all the dry ingredients in a bowl. Pour in the water and coconut oil and mix to a batter. Roll out the batter as thinly and evenly as possible between two sheets of baking parchment, then remove the top sheet and score the batter into squares.

Transfer the batter on the baking parchment to a cookie sheet and bake in the oven for 30–40 minutes, until golden brown. Let the bread cool and dry out before you break it into pieces.

Serve with boiled egg, red cabbage, bell peppers, arugula (rocket), and mayonnaise. See page 123 for recipe for mayonnaise.

Tips You could use buckwheat, sesame, amaranth, teff, almond, or hazelnut flour, for example, and it's fine to use either just one kind of flour or a mixture of several. You can also vary the mix of seeds to taste, as long as you stick to the basic recipe of ⅔ cups/100 g flour, ⅓ cup/165 g seeds, 1 cup/250 ml water, scant ¼ tsp/1.25 g herb salt, and 1 tbsp/15 ml coconut oil.

HAZELNUT BREAD

made with teff flour & buckwheat flakes

⅓ cup/50 g light teff flour
⅓ cup/50 g hazelnut flour
2 tsp/10 g psyllium husk
 fiber
1 tbsp/15 g baking powder
Generous ⅔ cup/65 g
 ground flaxseeds
Scant ¼ tsp/1.25 g herb salt
2 eggs
Generous ¾ cup/200 ml
 any milk
1 tbsp/15 ml coconut oil
 (room temperature)
Buckwheat flakes, for
 topping

Makes 1 loaf.

Preheat the oven to 390°F/200°C.

Combine all the dry ingredients in a bowl. Pour in the eggs, milk, and coconut oil and mix well.

Line a 2½-pint/1½-liter loaf pan with baking parchment and pour in the batter. Top with buckwheat flakes.

Bake in the oven for 50–60 minutes until the bread has a crisp crust.

Let cool on a wire rack before serving.

Tips   You can get hazelnut flour from well-stocked supermarkets or health food stores. Alternatively, you can grind it yourself in an almond mill or use a domestic food processor with a cutter attachment. You'll find teff flour in well-stocked supermarkets, health food stores, and online, or you can also use buckwheat, sesame, almond, or millet flour, for example.

CARROT BREAD

with apricot jam

Bread
¾ cup/110 g chickpea
  (garbanzo bean/gram) flour
¾ cup/110 g hazelnut flour
1 tbsp/15 g psyllium husk fiber
⅔ cup/90 g seeds, e.g.
  sunflower and pumpkin
  seeds
1 tsp/5 g baking powder
1 tsp/5 g baking soda
Pinch of ground cinnamon
2 tsp/5 g ground cumin
Scant ¼ tsp/1.25 g herb salt
2 eggs
⅔ cup/150 ml any milk
2 cups/100 g finely grated
  carrots

Topping
Pumpkin seeds
Sunflower seeds
Raisins
Sesame seeds

Apricot jam (makes
approx. 1 cup/350 ml)
⅔ cup/100 g dried apricots
1 small orange, divided into
  segments
Grated zest of 1 lemon
2 tbsp/30 ml lemon juice
Pinch of pure vanilla powder

Makes 1 loaf.

Preheat the oven to 390°F/200°C.

Combine all the dry ingredients, then mix in the eggs, milk, and carrots to form a thick, smooth batter. Let stand for 5 minutes.

Line a 2½-pint/1½-liter loaf pan with baking parchment and pour in the batter. Smooth the surface and sprinkle the bread with pumpkin seeds, sunflower seeds, raisins, or sesame seeds.

Bake in the oven for 50–60 minutes. Let cool completely on a wire rack before serving.

Place the apricots in a jar, top with water to cover, and refrigerate for at least 6 hours, preferably longer. Strain the soaking water from the apricots and reserve—it's good to use in smoothies, pastries, and sauces. Use a blender or hand blender to mix all the ingredients to a paste. The sweetness of the oranges can vary, so start off with 1 tbsp/15 ml of lemon juice and then add more, to taste.

Transfer to a glass jar and store in the refrigerator. Spread on the bread to serve.

Tips You can use quinoa, buckwheat, almond, sesame, millet, or amaranth flour in the bread. To give the marmalade a little extra zing, include ¼ tsp/1 g cinnamon and 1 tsp/5 g freshly grated ginger root.

ROSEHIP ROLLS

with sunflower seeds & pistachios

⅓ cup/50 g rosehip peel flour
⅓ cup/50 g quinoa flour
Scant ¼ tsp/1.25 g herb salt
2 tsp/10 g baking powder
2 tbsp/30 g psyllium husk fiber
Pinch of ground cinnamon
3 eggs
7 tbsp/100 ml any milk
1 tsp/5 ml honey
2 tbsp/30 ml olive oil

Topping
Sunflower seeds
Pistachios

Makes 5 rolls.

Preheat the oven to 350°F/175°C.

Combine all the dry ingredients, then add the eggs, milk, honey, and olive oil, and mix well. Let stand for 5 minutes.

Moisten your hands with a little cold water, shape five round rolls, and place them on a cookie sheet lined with baking parchment. Sprinkle on a few sunflower seeds and pistachios.

Bake on the middle shelf of the oven for 25–30 minutes; the loaves should have a crisp, golden crust. Let cool slightly before serving.

Tips As well as being incredibly tasty, rosehips are good for the skin, immune system, urinary tract, and digestion; they also contain loads of vitamin C. You'll find both rosehip peel flour and quinoa flour in some well-stocked specialty stores.

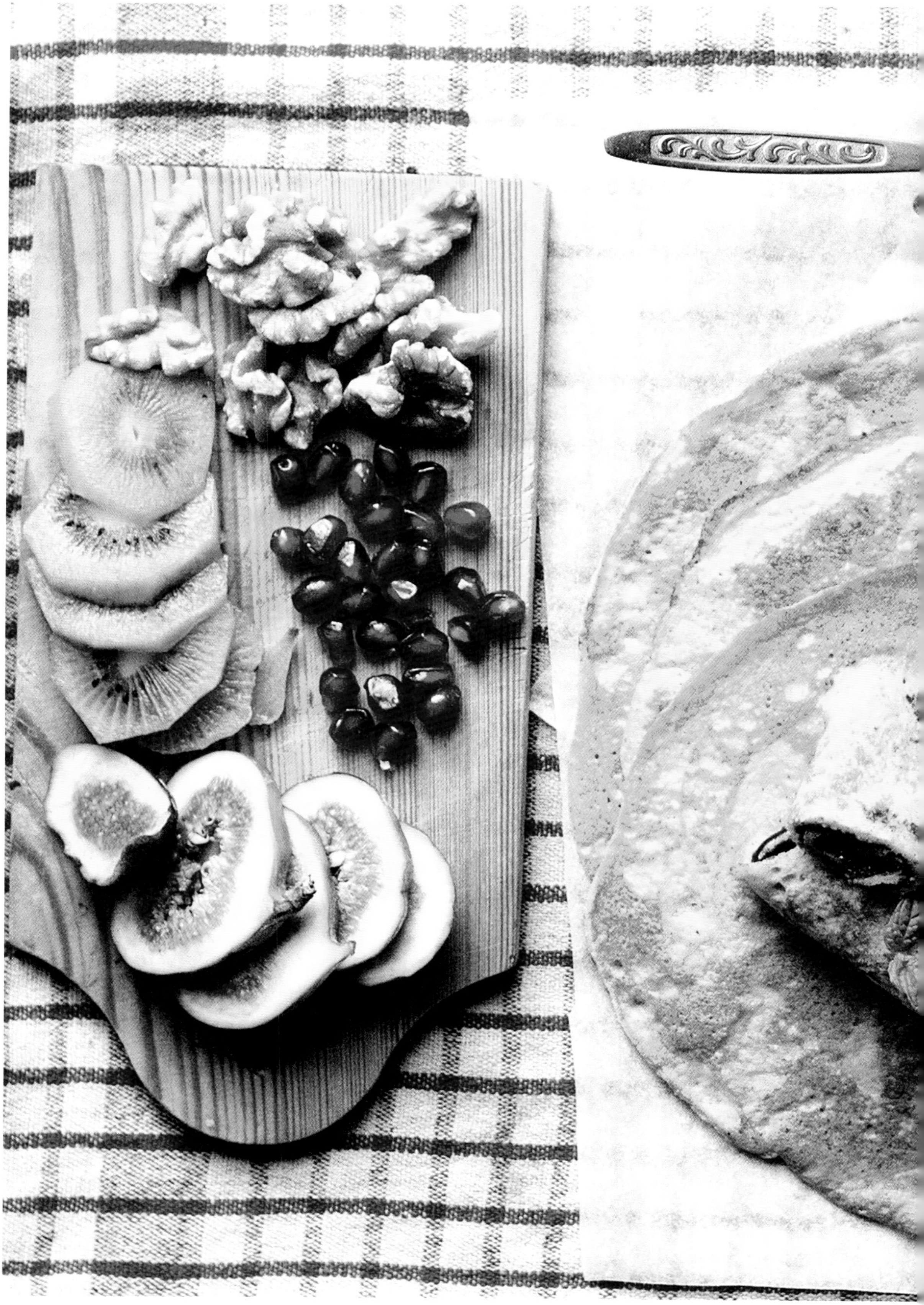

THIN PANCAKES

with the world's best & easiest nougat cream

Pancakes
6 tbsp/60 g buckwheat
  flour
½ tbsp/7.5 g psyllium husk
  fiber
Generous pinch of herb salt
Pinch pure vanilla powder
2 eggs
1 cup/250 ml any milk

Nougat cream
1 tbsp/15 g hazelnut butter
1 tbsp/15 ml coconut oil
1 tsp/5 g cocoa
1½ tsp/7.5 ml agave syrup

Topping options
Kiwi fruit
Walnuts
Fresh figs
Pomegranate seeds

Makes 5 pancakes.

Combine all the dry ingredients in a bowl and then whisk in the eggs and milk to make a smooth batter. Let stand for 15 minutes.

Heat a skillet to as hot as you can get it, add a little coconut oil, and reduce the heat to medium. Now fry the pancakes on both sides until they are golden brown. Dilute the batter with a little water if it seems too thick.

Combine the ingredients for the nougat cream in a saucepan. Heat over low heat until the mixture has a smooth consistency.

Pour the gently heated cream onto the pancakes straight from the saucepan. Kiwi fruit, walnuts, fresh figs, and pomegranate seeds make good toppings.

 Tips Agave syrup is a liquid sweetener extracted from the Mexican agave plant. The syrup is about 25 percent sweeter than sugar and has a caramel-like flavor. You can buy agave syrup in any well-stocked supermarket, health food store, or online.

CHIA PANCAKES

with berries & coconut chips

2 tbsp/20 g chia seeds
7 tbsp/100 ml any milk
Pinch of herb salt
Pinch of pure vanilla powder
2 eggs
3 tbsp/25 g coarse almond
   flour
1 tsp/5 g baking powder
½ tbsp/5 g psyllium husk
   fiber
Coconut oil, for frying

Topping options
Almond butter
Berries
Coconut chips
Pistachios

Makes about 5 pancakes, each 4 x 4 inches/10 x 10 cm.

Combine the chia seeds, milk, salt, and vanilla in a bowl. Stir well so that the chia seeds are completely immersed in the liquid. Let the mixture stand in the refrigerator for a few hours until it has reached a pudding-like consistency—you could even leave it overnight.

Now mix in the eggs, almond flour, baking powder, and psyllium husk fiber, and whisk until smooth. Let stand for 10–15 minutes and make small pancakes, frying for a few minutes on each side over medium heat.

Serve with almond butter, berries, coconut chips, and/or pistachios.

Tips   If the batter is too thick and difficult to manage, dilute it with a little drop more water before frying.

CRISPY WAFFLES

with pistachio cream & berries

Waffles
3 eggs
Generous ¾ cup/200 ml
  full-fat coconut milk
⅔ cup/150 ml water
2 tbsp/30 g almond butter
5 tbsp/75 ml coconut oil
½ cup/75 g quinoa flour
1 ½ tsp/7.5 g psyllium husk
  fiber
2 tsp/10 g baking powder
Scant ¼ tsp/1.25 g herb salt

Pistachio cream
(makes 1 cup/250 ml)
½ cup/65 g unsalted shelled
  pistachios
½ cup/115 g unsweetened
  apple sauce
1 tbsp/15 ml lemon or lime
  juice
½ banana
3½ tbsp/50 ml water

Makes about 8 waffles.

Whisk the eggs, coconut milk, water, and almond butter together until smooth.

Melt the coconut oil over low heat and pour it into the mixture. Combine the dry ingredients and whisk them into the liquid to make a thick and creamy batter. Let stand for 5–10 minutes.

Heat your waffle iron and lightly grease with coconut oil. Pour the thick batter into the iron and spread evenly. Cook the waffles until they are golden brown.

Mix the ingredients for the pistachio cream in a blender or with a hand blender until smooth and creamy.

If you have lots of guests or just a real craving for waffles, it is a good idea to preheat the oven to 300°F/150°C and keep the cooked waffles warm on a rack while you cook the rest of the batter.

Tips You can use other seed or nut butters in the batter, such as peanut, hazelnut, pistachio, or sunflower seed butter. These will make the waffles taste delicious.

CHICKPEA PANCAKES

with apples & toasted almonds

Pancakes
½ cup/75 g chickpea
    (garbanzo bean/gram)
    flour
4 eggs (room temperature)
1 tsp/5 g baking powder
1 cup/250 ml any milk
1 tbsp/15 ml agave syrup
Generous pinch of herb salt
Pinch of ground cardamom
¼ tsp/1 g ground cinnamon

1–2 apples
Coconut oil, for frying

Toasted almonds
3 tbsp/30 g almonds
Light coarse salt

Makes 20–25 pancakes.

Whisk all the pancake ingredients together in a bowl. It's a good idea to let the batter stand for 15–20 minutes, as it becomes even tastier and easier to use when frying.

In the meantime, core and thinly slice the apples.

Now chop the almonds and dry-fry them in a skillet, toasting over medium heat with a pinch of coarse salt. Set aside.

Cook the pancakes on a griddle greased with coconut oil or use a regular skillet. Pour the batter into the griddle or skillet and place a few of the thin apple slices on each pancake before flipping. Fry for a few minutes on each side on medium heat until they are golden brown.

Serve with toasted almonds.

Tips You can also make savory pancakes and serve them as finger food—top them off with a little avocado, red onion, dill, and lemon. Super tasty!

BLUEBERRY PANCAKES

made with quinoa flour

....

½ cup/75 g quinoa flour
Pinch of pure vanilla powder
Generous pinch of herb salt
1 tsp/5 g baking powder
1 tsp/5 g psyllium husk fiber
1 egg
⅔ cup/150 ml any milk
¾ cup/70 g blueberries
Coconut oil, for frying

Topping
Blueberries
Agave syrup

Makes 7 pancakes, each approx. 4 x 4 inches/10 x 10 cm.

Combine all the dry ingredients in a bowl and whisk in the eggs and milk to make a smooth batter. Let stand for 5 minutes, then stir in the blueberries.

Heat a skillet as hot as you can and add a little coconut oil. Reduce the heat to medium and fry the pancakes on both sides until they are golden brown. You may need to dilute the batter with a little water if it becomes too thick.

Top with some more blueberries and add a drizzle of agave syrup.

....

Tips   You could use other flours for the pancakes, for example buckwheat, chickpea, or nut flours. For egg substitutes, see page 11.

NUT MILK

with sweet dates & cinnamon

Scant 1 cup/130 g hazelnuts
2 cups/500 ml water
2 pitted dates
Generous pinch of ground
  cinnamon

Makes about 1⅔ cups/400 ml.

Using a blender or hand blender, mix the nuts, dates, and cinnamon with half the water, then stir in the remaining water. Let stand in the refrigerator for 2–3 hours and then strain the nut milk through cheesecloth.

Transfer the milk to a clean glass bottle and chill. It will keep for 2–3 days.

Tips   You can use this basic recipe with any nuts or seeds you like (almonds, cashews, pistachios, sunflower seeds, etc)—or you can make buckwheat milk by mixing in some buckwheat flakes. Leave out the dates and cinnamon if you prefer, or replace them with other flavors such as vanilla or cardamom.

BLUEBERRY SOUP

1 tbsp/10 g potato flour
3½ tbsp/50 ml water
¾ cup/70 g blueberries
¾ cup/70 g raspberries
2 tbsp/25 g coconut sugar
¼ tsp pure vanilla powder
1 tbsp/15 ml lemon juice

Serves 2.

Whisk the potato starch in cold water in a saucepan, then mix in the remaining ingredients. Place the pan on the heat and let the soup simmer, stirring until it thickens slightly.

Add a little more water if you don't want the soup to be too stodgy. If you prefer a thicker consistency, you can add more potato flour, but be sure to mix this with a little cold water before pouring it in; this will prevent any lumps from forming.

ROSEHIP SOUP

¾ tbsp/7.5 g potato flour
1 ⅔ cups/400 ml water
50 g rosehip seed flour
2 tbsp/25 g coconut sugar
1 tbsp/15 ml lemon juice
¼ tsp/1 g pure vanilla powder

Serves 2.

Follow exactly the same method as for blueberry soup.

Tips Coconut sugar is made from the nectar in coconut palm flowers. It has a slightly fruity flavor and a texture similar to raw sugar. One good tip is to serve the soup with a dollop of whipped coconut cream and some nuts that you have toasted in a dry pan. *Nyponsoppa* (rosehip soup) is a popular delicacy in Sweden.

CHOCOLATE SMOOTHIE

with cocoa nibs & a protein boost

1 tsp/5 g rice protein
Generous ¾ cup/200 ml
   any milk
1 tsp/5 g raw cocoa
1 small banana
½ avocado
1 tsp/5 ml lemon juice
Cocoa nibs, for garnishing

For a little extra boost
1 tsp/5 g carob powder
1 tsp/5 g maca powder

Serves 1.

Mix all ingredients except the cocoa nibs together in a blender or liquidize with a hand blender. Add a little carob and maca powder for an extra energy boost. Season to taste.

Pour into a glass and top with cocoa nibs.

Tips

The difference between raw cocoa and "regular" cocoa is that raw cocoa has not been heated above 104°F/40°C, which means the nutrients are preserved more effectively. Rice protein is a protein supplement that you'll find in health food stores or online. Carob powder is related to cocoa and has a lovely fruity flavor. The powder is very nutritious and may even have a settling effect on the stomach.

LINGONBERRY SMOOTHIE

with a tutti-frutti topping & a nettle boost

¾ cup/70 g cranberries
¾ cup/70 g raspberries
7 tbsp/100 ml full-fat
  coconut milk
7 tbsp/100 ml water
1 tsp/5 g nettle powder
1 tsp/5 ml agave syrup
1 tsp/5 ml lemon juice
1 tbsp/10 g pea protein
  powder

Topping options
Blackberries
Lingonberries
Sea-buckthorn berries
Blueberries
Red currants
Pistachios
Bee pollen

Serves 1–2.

Blend all the smoothie ingredients; you can use either frozen or fresh berries.

Pour into a bowl or a glass and top with berries, pistachios, and bee pollen.

Tips

Nettle powder is a mineral-filled compound that strengthens the body in many different ways, so boost your smoothie, juice, or porridge with a teaspoonful—green is good! Bee pollen consists of balls of pollen from plants that have been visited by bees. It is incredibly rich in amino acids and digestive enzymes, and is even said to have a positive effect on muscle formation and stamina. See note re bee pollen on page 2.

MANGO SMOOTHIE

with strawberries, chili & ginger

1 cup/140 g chopped fresh
  mango
⅔ cup/150 ml water
1 tbsp/10 g freshly grated
  ginger root
½ tsp/1 g finely chopped
  red chili
¼ cup/60 g chopped
  strawberries

Serves 1.

Liquidize the mango, water, ginger, and chilies to a smooth, fine consistency. Liquidize the strawberries to make a smooth, fine cream.

For an attractive effect, pour alternate layers into a glass.

Tips
Ginger's culinary and medicinal properties have been admired for thousands of years. This fine root has anti-inflammatory properties and may also help to combat nausea and other ailments.

STRAWBERRY SMOOTHIE

with lemon & cinnamon

....

1 cup/100 g frozen
   strawberries
7 tbsp/100 ml full-fat
   coconut milk
7 tbsp/100 ml water
Grated zest of ½ lemon
Pinch of ground cinnamon
½ tbsp/5 g pea protein

Serves 1.

Blend all the smoothie ingredients and season; you may
wish to dilute with a little more liquid to taste.

Pour into a glass and serve garnished with a little more
grated lemon zest.

....

Tips   If you leave out the water altogether and use only 3½ tbsp/50 ml coconut milk, you
will get a wonderfully creamy and gloriously soft ice-cream-like delight. Pea
protein is a protein supplement available from health food stores and online.

RASPBERRY SMOOTHIE

with fresh mint

½ banana
1 cup/100 g raspberries
Generous ¾ cup/200 ml
  any milk
Pinch of pure vanilla powder
Handful of fresh mint, leaves
  only
1 tsp/5 g rice protein

Makes 1 large glass.

Blend all the smoothie ingredients. You may need to dilute with a touch more liquid to reach the desired consistency.

Drink and enjoy!

 Tips To make a wonderful ice cream from the ingredients listed above, leave out the milk and use frozen raspberries and frozen banana. Blend until you have smooth, silky ice cream. Delicious! Rice protein is a protein supplement available from health food stores and online.

VANILLA GRANOLA

with crispy nuts & flakes

....

½ cup/55 g walnuts
3 tbsp/30 g hazelnuts
½ cup/65 g pistachios
¼ cup/30 g sunflower seeds
¼ cup/20 g buckwheat
  flakes
¼ cup/25 g millet flakes
⅓ cup/30 g coconut flakes
3 tbsp/30 g chia seeds
Generous pinch of pure
  vanilla powder
¼ tsp/1 g coarse salt
1 tbsp/15 ml melted coconut
  oil
1 tsp/5 ml agave syrup

Makes 2½ cups/600 ml.

Preheat the oven to 300°F/150°C.

Coarsely chop the nuts and mix with the remaining dry ingredients. Melt the coconut oil and agave syrup in a small saucepan, pour over the nut mixture, and stir in.

Spread the mixture onto a cookie sheet lined with baking parchment and bake in the oven for about 30 minutes or until golden, stirring 2 or 3 times.

Transfer the granola to a glass jar with a lid and store in a cool place to keep it fresh for longer.

....

Tips   Use any other nuts, seeds, or cereals you like. You might also like to try dried fruits, freeze-dried berries, rosehip peel flour, or have a go at flavoring it with cocoa etc.

BREAKFAST SALAD

with warmed vegetables

Salad
¼ bell pepper, finely sliced
4 zucchini (courgette) ba-
    tons, about 2 x 1 ¼ inches/
    5 x 3 cm
1 tsp/5 ml coconut oil, for
    frying
1 cup/30 g mixed salad—
    baby spinach and arugula
    (rocket), for example
½ avocado, sliced
2 cherry tomatoes

Topping
½ cup/15 g broccoli sprouts
¼–½ cup/50-100g hummus

Dressing
1 tsp/5 ml olive oil
1 tsp/5 ml lemon juice
Scant ¼ tsp/1.25 g herb salt

Serves 1.

Fry the bell peppers and zucchini (courgette) in coconut oil until golden brown. Arrange on a plate with the
mixed salad, avocado slices, and halved tomatoes. Pour
over the dressing and toss. Top with broccoli sprouts and
hummus.

See page 108 for hummus recipe.

Tips
Broccoli sprouts have high levels of a substance known as sulforaphane,
which has strong antioxidant properties; various studies have shown that
sulforaphane has a beneficial effect on the cells of our bodies—in other words,
they're real superfoods!

BUCKWHEAT BREAKFAST

with strawberries, banana & blueberries

....

½ cup/75 g whole grain
  buckwheat
1½ cups/350 ml water
Generous pinch of pure
  vanilla powder
Generous pinch of ground
  cinnamon
Generous pinch of herb salt

Topping options
Banana
Strawberries
Blueberries
Dried or fresh figs
Pumpkin seeds
Sunflower seeds

Serves 2.

Rinse the buckwheat, first in hot and then in cold water.

Bring the 1½ cups/350 ml water to a boil, add the buckwheat, salt, vanilla, and cinnamon, and cook for 10–15 minutes over low heat, stirring occasionally.

Let the grains swell up for a little while and serve with banana, strawberries, blueberries, and whichever milk you like. Top with some pumpkin and sunflower seeds.

....

Tips Buckwheat is a pseudocereal and is rich in minerals and protein. It is also incredibly kind to the stomach.

RASPBERRY PORRIDGE

with grated coconut & vanilla

1 tsp/5 g potato flour
5 tbsp/75 ml water
¾ cup/70 g raspberries
2 tbsp/20 g hazelnut flour
2 tbsp/10 g shredded
   coconut
Generous pinch of herb salt
Pinch of pure vanilla powder

Topping options
Chopped fruit
Nuts
Seeds
Bee pollen
Almond milk

Serves 1.

Mix the potato flour and the water in a saucepan. Stir in the remaining ingredients and bring to a boil, stirring until the porridge has a smooth and even texture.

Serve topped with chopped fruit, nuts, seeds, bee pollen, and almond milk.

Tips

You can replace the hazelnut flour with another nut or seed flour, such as almond flour. You can also replace the raspberries with other berries or mixed fruit, or even crack an egg into the porridge to make it more filling. See note on page 2 for bee pollen and bee allergies.

CHIA PUDDING

with hazelnut butter & berries

....

Pudding
4½ tbsp/50 g chia seeds
Generous ¾ cup/200 ml
    water
Generous pinch of pure
    vanilla powder
Generous pinch of herb salt
1 tsp/5 ml agave syrup
5 tbsp/75 ml full-fat coconut
    milk

Topping
Hazelnut butter
Raspberries
Blueberries
Kiwi fruit
Red currants
Sea-buckthorn berries

Serves 1–2.

Mix together all the ingredients except the coconut milk in a jar with a lid. Stir well so that the chia seeds are completely immersed in the liquid.

Place the lid on the jar and store in the refrigerator for about 3 hours, until the mixture has a pudding-like consistency—or let it stand overnight. The next morning, stir in 5 tbsp/75 ml coconut milk to make a creamy pudding. Add more coconut milk, if you wish, until you reach the consistency you want.

Serve with the toppings and your choice of milk—why not try almond milk? See page 46 for the recipe.

....

Tips   Chia seeds are one of the best sources of omega-3 fatty acids in the plant kingdom. They are rich in protein, carbohydrates, antioxidants, and fiber, and you can use them in baked goods, pancakes, chocolate, sprinkled on oatmeal and porridge, or in smoothies. If you don't soak them beforehand, it would be wise to remember to drink plenty of water. This pudding also makes a good dessert.

COCONUT PORRIDGE

cooked with millet flakes & berries

....

Generous ½ cup/50 g millet
    flakes
Generous ¾ cup/200 ml
    water
¼ cup/20 g shredded
    coconut
Pinch of pure vanilla powder
Generous pinch of herb salt

Topping options
Coconut chips
Blueberries
Lingonberries

Serves 1.

Mix all the ingredients together in a saucepan. Bring to a boil and simmer, stirring until you have a thick porridge.

Serve with coconut chips, berries, and your choice of milk—perhaps hazelnut or rice, for example.

....

Tips   Millet flakes are easy to digest and very rich in protein and fiber. They are a breeze to prepare and, above all, incredibly delicious. They are also very good when baked in bread, mixed into muesli, or used to thicken a sauce or soup. You can get them from well-stocked supermarkets or health food stores.

QUINOA PORRIDGE

cooked in coconut water

....

Scant ½ cup/75 g red quinoa
Generous ¾ cup/200 ml
  coconut water
Pinch of ground cinnamon
Generous pinch of herb salt

Topping options
Banana
Frozen berries
Pumpkin seeds
Grapes
Almonds
Passion fruit

Serves 1–2.

Rinse the quinoa in lukewarm water. Bring the coconut water to a boil in a saucepan and add the quinoa and cinnamon. Place a lid on the pan and simmer over low heat for about 15 minutes. Add the herb salt and let stand with the lid on for a few more minutes. The porridge is done when the quinoa has absorbed all the other ingredients.

Serve with your choice of milk and toppings; you could use hazelnut or rice milk.

....

Tips   Coconut water is available from well-stocked supermarkets, health food stores, and online. It is incredibly nutritious and often known as "Nature's sports drink." You could also use completely ordinary tap water. Quinoa has higher levels of protein than any other seed and it also contains useful fatty acids, minerals, and vitamins. You can also serve quinoa in salads or sauces, or with steaks etc.

BLUEBERRY PUDDING

with chia seeds & nut butter

5 tbsp/55 g chia seeds
Generous ¾ cup/200 ml
  any milk
¾ cup/70 g blueberries,
  fresh or frozen
Pinch of pure vanilla powder
½ tbsp/7.5 ml agave syrup
  (if required)
Pinch of herb salt

Topping options
Pumpkin seeds
Peanut butter
Blueberries
Bee pollen
Almond milk

Serves 1–2.

Mix all the ingredients together in a jar with a lid. Stir well so that the chia seeds are completely immersed in the liquid. Let stand for a few hours in the refrigerator until the pudding has achieved a thick consistency.

Serve with pumpkin seeds, peanut butter, blueberries, bee pollen, and almond milk.

Tips
You can usefully make this pudding in the evening and leave it in the refrigerator until morning—it's great for breakfast or as a snack to take to work.

NUT BUTTERS

wonderfully creamy & packed full of flavor

Hazelnut butter with a
hint of chocolate
Scant 1 cup/130 g raw
  hazelnuts
2 tsp/10 g raw cocoa
3 pitted dates
2 tbsp/30 ml coconut oil

Almond butter with
blueberries & cardamom
¾ cup + 2 tbsp/130 g raw
  sweet almonds
Generous pinch of ground
  cardamom
1 cup/100 g blueberries

Peanut butter
Scant 1 cup/140 g raw peanuts
½ tsp/2.5 g sea salt

Pistachio butter
1⅔ cups/200 g raw pistachios

Cashew nut butter with
raspberry and vanilla
⅔ cup/100 g raw cashew nuts
1 cup/100 g raspberries
Generous pinch of pure
  vanilla powder

Makes about ¾–1 cup/200 ml of each kind of nut butter.

The following applies to all the nut butters.

Mix the nuts at top speed in a food processor until you have a smooth, fine butter; this will take 10–20 minutes, depending on your food processor and the variety of nut. Now add the flavoring and carry on mixing.

Transfer the nut butter to a clean glass jar with a lid and store in the refrigerator. It will keep for about a week.

Obviously, all the extra flavorings are optional and you can keep all these nut butters plain if you prefer.

Tips
Peanut butter is wonderfully good on pancakes, in smoothies, as a sauce base, as a baking ingredient, in ice cream, or just eaten straight from the jar. And it's super easy! You can also make butter with seeds, such as sunflower, flax, hemp, or pumpkin seeds.

CHIA JAM

with blueberries, raspberries & mango

....

Base recipe
3½ tbsp/37.5 g chia seeds
⅔ cup/150 ml water

Blueberry flavor
1 cup/100 g blueberries
Pinch of ground cardamom
Pinch of pure vanilla powder
1 tsp/5 ml lemon juice
1 tsp/5 ml agave syrup

Raspberry flavor
1 cup/100 g raspberries
Pinch of pure vanilla powder
1 tsp/5 ml lemon juice
1 tsp/5 ml agave syrup

Mango flavor
⅔ cup/100 g mango
Grated zest of ½ lime
Pinch of pure vanilla powder
1 tsp/5 ml lemon juice
1 tsp/5 ml agave syrup

Makes about ⅔ cup/150 ml jam of each flavor.

Mix the chia seeds and water in a bowl. Stir well so that the chia seeds are completely immersed in the liquid. Let stand for 5–10 minutes.

When the chia seeds have formed a thick jelly in the water, divide the mixture among three bowls and add the ingredients for the various jam flavors to their respective bowls. Use a blender or hand blender to mix up the jam.

Transfer the jam to jars with screw-top lids and store in the refrigerator for a little while until they have settled to a smooth consistency. The jam will keep for about a week in the refrigerator.

Serve on toasted bread or seed crispbreads, stir into porridge, or eat it as it is!

....

Tips   Chia seeds are good for people looking for a natural method of blood glucose regulation, athletes trying to boost their stamina, or anyone who just wants to eat well and stay healthy.

CREAMY CHEESE SPREAD

made from cashew nuts

Sun-dried tomato & oregano

Scant ⅔ cup/90 g cashews
3 sundried tomatoes in oil, drained
Scant ½ cup/50 g nutritional yeast
1½ tbsp/25 ml water
¾ tsp/3.75 g herb salt
1 small clove of garlic
Pinch cayenne pepper
Generous pinch of turmeric
½ tsp/2.5 ml honey
1 tbsp/15 ml lemon juice
3½ tbsp/50 ml coconut oil (room temperature)
1 tsp/5 g dried oregano + 2 tbsp/30 g to garnish

Makes about 1 cup/250 g.

Place the cashew nuts in a jar and pour over water to cover the nuts. Put on the lid and let stand overnight in the refrigerator. The next day, pour away the water.

Mix all the ingredients at top speed in a food processor for about 2–3 minutes until you have a smooth, fine paste. Every so often, push down any nuts sticking to the side.

Transfer to a sheet of baking parchment and roll into a smooth and finely textured log. Let stand in the refrigerator overnight.

Remove the baking parchment and roll the cheese in 2 tbsp/30 g oregano.

Cilantro (coriander) & lemon

Scant 1 cup/125 g raw cashew nuts
⅔ cup/75 g nutritional yeast
1 tbsp/15 ml lemon juice
1 tsp/5 g herb salt
½ tsp/2.5 g dried thyme
½ tsp/2.5 g dried basil
½ tsp/2.5 g dried cilantro (coriander)
1½ tbsp/25 ml water
3 tbsp/30 g whole, peeled, white sesame
  seeds

Makes about 1 cup/200 g.

Mix all the ingredients except the sesame seeds at top speed in a food processor for about 2–3 minutes until you have a smooth, fine paste. Every so often, push down any nuts sticking to the side.

Moisten your hands in cold water and shape the cheese into a smooth, finely textured pattie. Wrap in a sheet of baking parchment and let stand in the refrigerator for a few hours to let it settle, preferably overnight.

Remove the baking parchment and roll the cheese in some sesame seeds.

Tips The cheese will keep for a week in the refrigerator, but will also freeze well. You'll find nutritional yeast in health food stores or online. These spreads are also delicious with BBQ, as a tasty addition to salad, as a sauce, or just eaten as it is on seed crispbread.

LUNCH
&
DINNER

CHILI-LIME BURGERS

with dressing & soft cashew buns

Cashew buns
3 eggs
½ tsp/2.5 g herb salt
⅔ cup/150 g cashew nut butter
1 tsp/5 ml apple cider vinegar
2 egg whites
1 tsp/5 g psyllium husk fiber
2 tsp/10 g baking powder
Coconut oil, for the molds
Peeled sesame seeds, to garnish

Dressing (makes about 7 tbsp/100 ml)
1 tbsp/15 ml full-fat coconut milk
4 tbsp/60 g tomato paste
1 small clove of garlic, pressed
¼ tsp/1.25 g sea salt
Scant ½ tsp/2 g cayenne pepper
1 tbsp/15 ml agave syrup
1 tsp/5 ml lime juice

Burgers
Scant 4 cups/285 g cooked soybeans
Generous 2 cups/160 g cooked black lentils
1 clove of garlic
1½–2 tsp/7.5–10 g sea salt
1¼ inch/3 cm red chili, finely chopped
3½ tbsp/50 ml water
Grated zest of 1 lime
1 tsp/5 ml lime juice
1½ tsp/7.5 g psyllium husk fiber
Coconut oil, for frying

Makes 6 burgers.

Place an ovenproof bowl of water at the bottom of the oven (to give the bread a better color and crust) and preheat the oven to 350°F/175°C.

Mix together the 3 eggs, salt, and nut butter, then add the cider vinegar. Beat the egg whites until stiff, then whisk the psyllium husk fiber and baking powder into the egg and nut mixture and fold in the egg whites. Transfer the batter to 6 large muffin cups greased with coconut oil. Smooth down the tops and garnish with sesame seeds.

Bake for 18–20 minutes. Let the buns cool slightly on a wire rack and remove from the molds.

Meanwhile, mix the dressing ingredients together and place in the refrigerator. Mix all the ingredients for the burgers except the psyllium husk fiber with a hand blender or in a food processor. Add the psyllium husk fiber, continue mixing, and then let stand for 5–10 minutes.

Moisten your hands in cold water and form the mixture into 6 patties. Heat plenty of coconut oil in a skillet and fry the burgers over medium heat until golden brown. Serve with the buns, dressing, and vegetables, such as cucumbers, red onions, bell peppers, and arugula.

Tips
You can also use other nut creams or seed butters to make bread—try sunflower seed, almond, pumpkin seed, or peanut butter. The avocado dip on page 117 is also a treat with this burger. Try chickpeas or mung beans, for example, to make the burger patties.

SWEET POTATO FRIES

with creamy basil quinoa

Sweet potato fries
1 medium sweet potato
Generous pinch of cayenne
 pepper
Generous pinch of paprika
½ tsp/2.5 g herb salt
½ tsp/2.5 g garlic powder

**Basil cream (makes
generous ¾ cup/200 ml)**
Scant ¼ cup/40 g white
 quinoa
7 tbsp/100 ml water
1 avocado
Large handful of fresh basil
1 tbsp/15 ml lemon juice
1 tsp/5 ml agave syrup
Scant ¼ tsp/1.25 g herb salt
Pinch of black pepper

Makes 1–2 servings.

Preheat the oven to 440°F/225°C.

Wash and scrub the sweet potato carefully. I make my fries with the skin on, but you can peel the potato if you prefer. Cut into batons, place on a baking tray lined with baking parchment, and season with cayenne pepper, paprika powder, herb salt, and garlic powder.

Bake in the oven for 30–40 minutes or until crisp and golden.

In the meantime, boil the quinoa in the water until it is soft (about 10 minutes). Let cool, then mix with the avocado, basil, lemon juice, agave syrup, and salt and pepper. It's ready to serve and savor!

Tips Sweet potatoes are also wonderful puréed, mashed into patties, added to soups, or baked in bread and cakes. They may even have an anti-inflammatory effect on the body.

PIZZA

with tomato sauce & vegetables

Tomato sauce
1 small yellow onion, finely
  chopped
1–2 cloves of garlic, pressed
1 tbsp/15 ml coconut oil
1 cup/200 g chopped fresh
  tomatoes
Scant ½ cup/100 g tomato
  paste
2 tbsp/30 ml agave syrup
1 tsp/5 g herb salt
Pinch of cayenne pepper
1–2 tbsp/5–10 g oregano,
  dried or fresh

Pizza
7 tbsp/70 g peeled white
  sesame seeds
½ cup/75 g light teff flour
1 tbsp/15 g psyllium husk
  fiber
1 tsp/5 g baking powder
½ tsp/2.5 g herb salt
3 eggs
7 tbsp/100 ml any milk

Makes 2 medium pizzas or 1 large pizza.

Preheat the oven to 440°F/225°C.

First up is the tomato sauce: sweat the onion and garlic in coconut oil in a saucepan, then add the chopped tomatoes, tomato paste, agave syrup, and spices. Simmer until you have a thick tomato sauce, stirring occasionally. Let the sauce cool.

Mix all the dry ingredients for the pizza together, then mix in the milk and eggs to make a batter. Let stand for 5 minutes.

Line a baking tray with baking parchment and, using a spatula, spread the batter to form two round pizzas—or fill one large cookie sheet with all the batter. Bake on the middle shelf of the oven for 10–12 minutes.

Remove the pizza and add the tomato sauce and optional toppings. Return to the oven for another 10–15 minutes.

Suggested toppings include vegetables, mixed beans, onion, garlic, banana, pineapple, curry powder, sesame seeds... The more the merrier, in my opinion!

 Tips Light teff flour, buckwheat flour, sesame flour, quinoa flour, and chickpea flour are all good options for pizza batter. I think that a mixture of two flours tastes best, but you don't need any more than one to make a successful batter. Give it a try and discover your favorite!

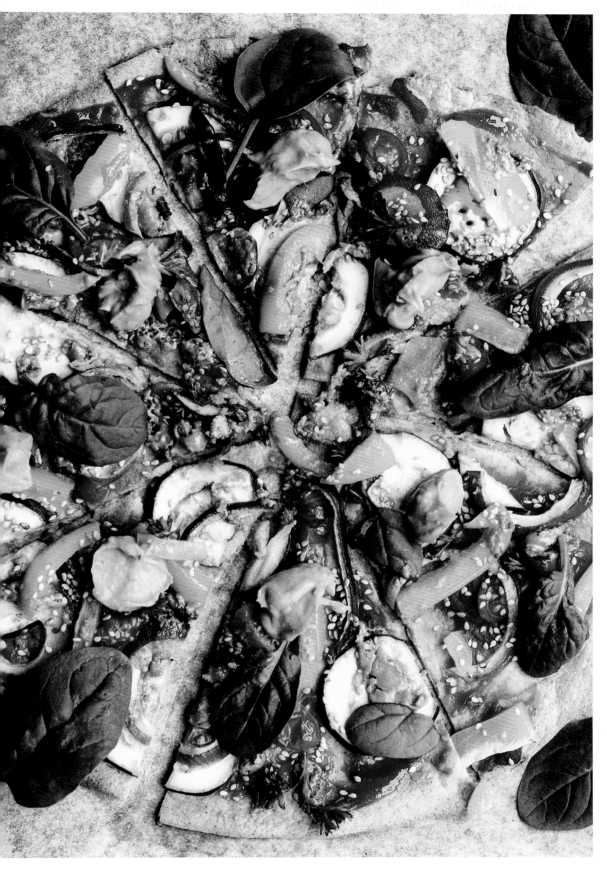

CRISPY NUTBALLS

with orange salad & walnuts

Nutballs

5 tbsp/40 g sunflower seeds
2 tbsp/30 ml coconut oil
   (room temperature)
2 tbsp/30 g nut butter,
   e.g. almond or pistachio
1 clove of garlic
1 tsp/5 g of chia seeds
1 tsp/5 g psyllium husk fiber
¼ tsp/1.25 g herb salt
¾ tsp/3.75 g ground cumin
1½ tbsp/22.5 ml lemon juice
1 tsp/5 ml agave syrup
Pumpkin and sunflower
   seeds, for coating
Coconut oil, for frying

Salad

2 cups/60 g mixed salad, e.g.
   rocket (arugula) and baby
   spinach
2 cherry tomatoes
¼ red onion
1–2 tbsp/15–30 g
   pomegranate seeds
½ segmented orange
4–5 walnuts

Dressing

1 tsp/5 ml olive oil
1 tsp/5 ml lemon juice
Scant ¼ tsp/1.25 g herb salt

Makes 1 serving of 5 nutballs.

Using a food processor, whizz the sunflower seeds to a coarse flour, then add the remaining ingredients for the nutballs and mix to a smooth, finely textured batter. Let stand for 20 minutes. Mix a little more.

Moisten your hands with a few drops of cold water and shape the 5 nutballs. Roll these in pumpkin seeds and then place in the refrigerator for about 20 minutes to relax.

Now fry the nutballs in a little coconut oil over medium heat. Make sure the surface has turned a golden color before turning them in the pan—this will make them easier to handle. If you turn them too quickly, the pumpkin seeds can easily fall off.

Serve with the salad and dressing.

 Tips Enjoy the nutballs raw, without frying them—this is at least as good and also handy if you are short of time. If you don't have any nut butters in the house, you can use an extra 4 tbsp/30 g of sunflower seeds: process all the sunflower seeds to make a butter instead of a coarse flour, then add the remaining ingredients.

FALAFEL WRAP

with soft bread & dressing

Bread
1 tbsp/10 g peeled white sesame seeds
3 tbsp/25 g quinoa flour
¾ tbsp/12.5 g psyllium husk fiber
½ tsp/2.5 g baking soda
Pinch of turmeric
½ tsp/2.5 g herb salt
1 egg
⅓ cup/75 ml any milk

Falafel
2¼ cups/165 g cooked chickpeas
  (garbanzo beans)
1 clove of garlic
½ cup/12 g fresh chopped parsley
1 tsp/5 g ground cumin
3 tbsp/45 ml lemon juice
2 tbsp/30 ml coconut oil (room
  temperature)
4 tbsp/40 g chickpea (garbanzo
  bean/gram) or sesame flour
½–1 tsp/2.5–5 g herb salt
Sesame seeds, for coating
Coconut oil, for frying

Dressing
6 tbsp/90 ml coconut cream
2 tsp/10 g tomato paste
Scant ¼ tsp/1.25 g herb salt
1 clove of garlic, pressed
1 tsp/5 ml honey
2 tsp/10 ml lemon juice

Serves 1–2.

Preheat the oven to 440°F/225°C.

Mix together all the dry ingredients for the bread in a bowl, then whisk in the milk and eggs to make a batter. Line a baking sheet with baking parchment and spread a thin layer of the batter on top. Bake in the oven for 7–8 minutes, remove, and let cool on a wire rack.

Combine all the ingredients for the falafel and let stand for 5 minutes. Moisten your hands with a little cold water and shape into 12 balls, then roll these in the sesame seeds. Fry in coconut oil in a skillet, making sure they have a golden crust all over. Beware of using too much coconut oil in the pan—this may cause the sesame seeds to fall off.

Mix together all the ingredients for the dressing in a bowl. Chill and let stand until you serve.

Place the falafel and vegetables of your choice on the bread. Drizzle over the dressing and roll up.

Tips   You can use buckwheat or amaranth flour, for example, for the bread, and you can leave out the sesame seeds.

RED BEET STEAKS

with sweet potato & chilled coconut almond sauce

Red beet steaks
2¼ cups/170 g cooked
   chickpeas (garbanzo beans)
Generous 1 cup/230 g
   cooked red beets (beetroot)
¾ tsp/3.75 g herb salt
1½ tsp/7.5 g psyllium husk
   fiber
1 clove of garlic

Coconut almond sauce
5 tbsp/75 ml full-fat
   coconut milk
1 tbsp/15 g almond butter
¼ tsp/1.25 g herb salt
1 tsp/5 ml lemon juice
½ tsp/2.5 g garlic powder

Accompaniments
Cooked sweet potato
Fresh thyme
Seed crispbread, recipe on
   page 23

Serves 1–2.

Preheat the oven to 440°F/225°C. Mix all the ingredients for the steaks in a food processor or in a bowl using a hand blender.

Shape the mixture into 4–6 patties, line a baking tray with baking parchment, brush with a thin layer of coconut oil, and place the patties on top.

Bake for 15–20 minutes, turning halfway through.

Combine the sauce ingredients in a bowl and keep in the refrigerator until you are ready to serve.

Serve the steaks with boiled sweet potatoes, coconut almond sauce, fresh thyme, and seed crispbreads.

Tips Use any other nut or seed butter of your choice in the sauce. Pistachio butter works surprisingly well if you are making this as a main dish, or you might prefer sunflower seed butter or tahini. Tahini is a sesame seed paste that is available in most most well-stocked supermarkets or health food stores.

HOTPOT

with avocado & crisp red cabbage

Hotpot
1 red onion, finely chopped
1 clove of garlic, finely chopped
2½ cups/200 g cooked chickpeas
   (garbanzo beans)
2½ cups/200 g cooked kidney
   beans
Coconut oil, for frying
1 cup/250 ml full-fat coconut milk
1¾ cups/350 g crushed tomatoes
   (fresh or canned)
2 tbsp/30 ml agave syrup
1 tbsp/15 g curry powder
1 tsp/5 g Herbamare herb salt
Generous pinch of cayenne pepper
1 tsp/5 g ground ginger
1 tsp/5 g ground cumin
Pinch of ground cinnamon

Topping options
Cashews
Sesame seeds
Spinach leaves
Avocado
Red cabbage

Zesty sauce
7 tbsp/100 ml coconut cream
½ tsp/2.5 ml honey
1 tbsp/15 ml lemon juice
Grated zest of ¼ lemon

Serves 4.

Fry the onion, garlic, chickpeas (garbanzo beans), and kidney beans in coconut oil in a casserole dish, then add the coconut milk, crushed tomatoes, and spices. Let simmer for a little while to allow the flavors to mingle—the longer the better.

Check the flavor and adjust the seasoning to taste. Top with, for example, cashew nuts, sesame seeds, spinach, avocado, and red cabbage and serve with the sauce.

Tips This hotpot is perfect if you are cooking for several guests. It's a favorite with most people. Add a handful of raisins to the pan as a variation.

FISH CURRY

with peanut butter & crunchy vegetables

Approx. 14 oz/400 g white
  fish fillets
1 onion, finely chopped
3 cloves of garlic, pressed
Coconut oil, for frying
3⅓ cups/800 ml full-fat
  coconut milk
3 tbsp/45 g peanut butter
1½ tsp/7.5 g curry powder
2–2½ tsp/10–12.5 g herb salt
3 tbsp/45 ml lemon juice
1 tbsp/15 ml honey
Generous pinch of turmeric
1½ bell peppers
¼ broccoli head
Boiled sweet potatoes,
  if liked

Serves 2–4.

Cut the fish into small dice. Brown the onion and garlic in coconut oil in a large cast-iron pot, then add the fish, coconut milk, peanut butter, and spices, and simmer for 15–20 minutes.

Slice the peppers and broccoli.

Add the vegetables and if (like me) you like them crunchy, cook for a minute before serving, otherwise simmer a little while longer.

This stew is excellent served with boiled sweet potatoes.

Tips Choose a fish variety that is MSC-certified and organic. Lentils or beans are a good vegetable alternative to fish, and you can leave out the peanut butter if you like.

HOT LENTIL SOUP

with refreshing lemon cream

Soup

2¼ cups/450 g uncooked
  or 13 cups/1 kg cooked red
  lentils
7 tbsp/100 ml full-fat
  coconut milk
Generous ¾ cup/150 g
  chopped tomatoes (fresh
  or canned)
1½ tsp/7.5 g cumin
Generous pinch of ground
  cinnamon
1½ tsp/7.5 g curry
1 tsp/5 g turmeric
1½ tbsp/15 g grated fresh
  ginger root
Herb salt, to taste
¼ tsp/1.25 g cayenne pepper
2 tbsp/30 ml lemon juice
3 cloves of garlic, pressed
2 tbsp/30 ml agave syrup
Generous ¾ cup/200 ml
  water
Parsley, for garnishing

Lemon cream (makes generous ¾ cup/200 ml)

¾ cup/200 ml coconut
  cream
Grated zest of 1 lemon
2 tbsp/30 ml lemon juice
Generous pinch of herb salt

Serves 4–6.

Rinse the uncooked lentils in a sieve and place in a saucepan with plenty of water. Put the lid on and simmer over low heat for about 10 minutes. Keep an eye on the pan, as these can easily boil over.

The lentils are done when they have gone soft and mushy. Pour off any excess water. (If you are using precooked lentils, you can skip this step.)

Now stir in the coconut milk, chopped tomatoes, spices, and agave syrup, and simmer for a few minutes so the flavors can come into their own.

In the meantime, combine the ingredients for the lemon cream in a bowl.

Blend the soup in a blender or with a hand blender and dilute to the consistency you like with water. Season with salt, sprinkle with parsley, and serve with the lemon cream.

 Tips Several studies have shown turmeric to have anti-inflammatory properties for joints, muscles, and organs. It also contains very strong dyes, so be careful to protect your clothes when you use it.

HUMMUS
with ginger & honey

2 cups/135 g cooked
   chickpeas (garbanzo
   beans)
3 tbsp/45 ml olive oil
Juice of ½ lemon
Herb salt, to taste
Pinch of cayenne pepper
½ tsp/0.75 g freshly grated
   ginger root
1 clove of garlic, pressed
2 tbsp/30 ml water
2 tbsp/30 ml tahini
   (optional)
1½ tsp/7.5 ml honey
Parsley, for garnishing

Makes 1 cup/250 ml.

Place all the ingredients in a bowl and mix with a hand blender, adding water and olive oil until the desired consistency is reached. Add a little more seasoning if required, sprinkle with parsley, and drizzle with a little olive oil.

Tips Hummus is good to eat as it is, as a dip for vegetables or as a sauce for a main course. It goes well with tapas, on bread, or in a salad.

CREAMY DIPS

served on zucchini & eggplant

Bell pepper dip
2 red bell peppers
1 tbsp/15 ml coconut oil
Generous 1 cup/80 g cooked
   soybeans
½ clove of garlic
1½ tsp/7.5 ml olive oil
Herb salt, to taste

**Sweet 'n' savory
curry dip**
2¼ cups/170 g cooked
   chickpeas (garbanzo
   beans)
1½ tsp/7.5 ml olive oil
Herb salt, to taste
¼ tsp/1.25 g curry powder
1 clove of garlic
2 tbsp/30 ml water
1½ tsp/7.5 ml honey

1 zucchini (courgette), sliced
1 eggplant (aubergine), sliced
Coconut oil, for frying

Makes about ¾ cup/200 ml of each dip.

Slice the peppers and fry for a few minutes in coconut oil until soft.

Using a hand blender, mix the ingredients in a separate bowl for each dip. Season with additional spices to taste.

Fry the zucchini (courgette) and eggplant (aubergine) slices in a little coconut oil until they are soft and golden brown.

Serve with the dips!

Tips Dips are a very good accompaniment to a main course, as a spread on bread, or eaten as they are as a snack. You can substitute nuts and seeds for the soybeans and chickpeas.

SPRING ROLLS

with vegetables & mango dip

Mango dip
4 tbsp/60 g almond or
  cashew nut butter
1 cup/140 g finely chopped
  fresh mango
1 tsp/1.5 g freshly grated
  ginger root
1 clove of garlic, pressed
Generous pinch of cayenne
  pepper
Scant ¼ tsp/1.25 g herb salt,
  or more to taste
2 tbsp/30 ml water (if
  required)

Spring rolls
1 carrot
½ bell pepper
¼ cucumber
½ avocado
1 scallion
5 pieces of rice paper
Large handful of fresh
  cilantro (coriander)
½ lime, to squeeze over
Herb salt, to taste

Makes 5 rolls.

Whizz all the ingredients for the mango dip in a blender or liquidize with a hand blender. Add 2 tbsp/30 ml water if required to get the consistency you want. Season to taste.

Cut all the vegetables into batons and chop the scallions finely.

Bring a large pot of water to a boil, set aside, and let cool slightly. Soak a piece of rice paper in the warm water for about 10 seconds until soft.

Place the rice paper on a clean, damp paper towel and fill with the vegetables, onions, and cilantro (coriander). Squeeze over the lime juice and season. Fold in both ends of the rice paper after rolling up into a neat packet.

Repeat with the remaining pieces of rice paper. Soak one piece of paper at a time; if they are in the water too long, they can easily break up.

Serve the spring rolls with mango dip.

Tips   It's incredibly easy to vary these spring rolls by filling them with other things you like. If you wish, you can also fry them briefly in coconut oil to give them a light crust.

TACO WRAPS

1½ tbsp/15 g buckwheat flour
1½ tbsp/7.5 g psyllium husk fiber
Scant ¼ tsp/1.25 g herb salt
1 egg
½ cup/125 ml water

Makes 2 large or 4 small wraps.

Preheat the oven to 440°F/225°C.

Combine the dry ingredients. Whisk in the eggs and then add water to make a smooth, finely textured batter. Let stand for about 7 minutes: the batter should have a creamy consistency. Line a cookie sheet with baking parchment and, using a spatula, spread out the batter to make 2 large or 4 small wraps (you may need to dip the spatula in cold water every so often). Try to distribute the batter as evenly as possible and avoid having any holes. Place on the middle shelf of the oven and bake for 5–6 minutes. Let cool before removing them from the paper.

If you want to make several batches of wraps, the smartest approach is to make another lot of batter while the previous wraps are baking, rather than making a large amount at once. This is because the psyllium husk fiber constantly absorbs and locks in more liquid the longer it is allowed to stand, and can therefore get a bit stodgy if it is left too long.

Tips You can also use quinoa or chick-pea (garbanzo bean) flour, for example, for the wraps.

TOMATO SALSA

1½ cups/300 g crushed fresh tomatoes
1 tsp/5 g herb salt
1 tbsp/15 ml agave syrup or honey
1 clove of garlic, pressed
Generous pinch of cayenne pepper
1 tbsp/3 g finely chopped fresh cilantro (coriander)

Makes 2 cups/250 ml.

Place all the salsa ingredients in a pan and simmer for about 10 minutes; the longer you cook it, the tastier it will become.

Transfer the salsa to a bowl and let cool.

Tips You can leave out the herbs or replace it with another seasoning if you wish.

AVOCADO DIP

1 avocado
2 tbsp/30 ml full-fat coconut milk
2 tbsp/30 ml lime juice
Herb salt, to taste
1 small clove of garlic, pressed
½–1 inch/1-2 cm red chili, finely chopped
  or
Pinch of cayenne pepper

Makes 1⅔ cups/200 ml.

Mix all the ingredients for the dip in a blender or with a hand blender, season to taste, and serve.

TACO CHIPS

6 tbsp/60 g buckwheat flour
  + ½ tbsp/5 g for dusting
3 tbsp/25 g chickpea flour
½ tsp/2.5 g bicarbonate of soda
1 tsp/5 g ground cumin
Pinch of cayenne pepper
½ tsp/2.5 g garlic powder
1 tsp/5 g of coarse salt
Pinch of turmeric
2 egg whites
1 tbsp/15 ml coconut oil (room
  temperature)

Preheat the oven to 300°F/150°C. Combine all the dry ingredients in a bowl. Add the egg whites and coconut oil and mix to a batter. Sprinkle with ½ tbsp/5 g of buckwheat flour and let rise for 15–20 min.

Divide the batter in two and roll out one half in a thin layer between 2 sheets of baking parchment; make sure you roll it evenly so that the baking time will be the same across the whole sheet. Remove the top sheet of paper and score the batter into taco-shaped triangles with a knife so that you can easily separate them when they have finished baking.

Bake the chips on the top shelf of the oven for 20–25 minutes, until they are crunchy. Remove and let cool on a wire rack. Separate out the individual chips, then repeat the process with the other half of the batter.

Tips This dip also works incredibly well as a sauce on a burger, as dressing for a salad, or on bread.

Tips You can also use sesame, coarse-ground almond, or amaranth flour, for example, for these chips.

VEGETABLE LASAGNA
with chickpea sauce & spinach leaves

Lasagna sheets
2 tbsp/20 g quinoa flour
1½ tsp/7.5 g psyllium husk fiber
½ tsp/2.5 g baking soda
Scant ¼ tsp/1.25 g herb salt
Pinch of turmeric (optional)
½ cup/125 ml water
2 eggs, at room temperature
Coconut oil for brushing

Tomato sauce
¼ red onion, finely chopped
1 large clove of garlic, finely
  chopped
½ cup/25 g shredded carrots
1 tbsp/15 ml coconut oil
1 cup/200 g chopped fresh
  tomatoes
1 tbsp/15 ml agave syrup
Herb salt and pepper

Chickpea sauce
2 cups/135 g cooked
  chickpeas (garbanzo beans)
6 tbsp/40 g walnuts
1 large bunch fresh basil
Herb salt and pepper
¼ tsp/1.25 g garlic powder
7 tbsp/100 ml any milk
1 tbsp/15 ml olive oil

Vegetable layers
½ zucchini (courgette)
1¼ cups/50 g spinach leaves

Serves 2–3.

Preheat the oven to 440°F/225°C.

Combine all the dry ingredients for the lasagna sheets. Whisk in the water and eggs and mix to a smooth batter. Let stand for 7–10 minutes; the batter should have a creamy consistency. Line a cookie sheet with baking parchment and brush with a thin layer of coconut oil. Using a spatula (dipped occasionally in cold water), spread the batter to make a layer 16 x 12 inches/40 x30 cm. Try to distribute the batter as evenly as possible, so the sheets don't have any holes. Place on the middle shelf of the oven, bake for 5–6 minutes, and let cool. Cut the sheet into four rectangular pieces, each 4 x 12 inches/10 x 30 cm. If you want to make more lasagna sheets, make some more batter while the last batch is baking. The psyllium husk fiber constantly absorbs and locks in more liquid the longer it is allowed to stand, and can therefore get a bit stodgy if it is left too long.

Reduce the heat to 390°F/200°C. Sweat the onion, garlic, and carrots in coconut oil in a saucepan, then add the tomatoes, agave syrup, salt, and pepper, and simmer for 10–15 minutes. Liquidize with a hand blender if necessary. Liquidize the ingredients for the chickpea sauce and set aside. Slice the zucchini (courgette) with a cheese slicer.

Line a 2½-pint/1½-liter loaf pan with baking parchment and fill with alternating layers of lasagna sheets, zucchini (courgette), spinach, tomato sauce, and chickpea sauce. Bake in the oven for about 20 minutes.

Tips You can use chickpea or buckwheat flour for the lasagna sheets and you can substitute sunflower seeds, for example, for the walnuts in the chickpea sauce.

VEGETABLE WRAPS
with curry hummus & honey mayonnaise

Wraps
1½ tbsp/15 g buckwheat flour
1½ tsp/7.5 g psyllium husk fiber
Scant ¼ tsp/1.25 g herb salt
1 egg
½ cup/125 ml water

Honey mayonnaise
(makes 7 tbsp/100 ml)
1 egg yolk
½ tsp/2.5 g French mustard
Approx. 7 tbsp/100 ml rapeseed oil
1½ tbsp/22.5 ml lemon juice
½ tsp/2.5 ml grated lemon zest
1 tbsp/15 ml honey
Pinch of cayenne pepper
Pinch of garlic powder
Herb salt, to taste

Curry hummus
(makes 1 ⅓ cups/400 ml)
4⅔ cups/350 g cooked chickpeas
3 tbsp/45 ml olive oil
Herb salt, to taste
1 tbsp/15 ml lemon juice
1 small clove of garlic
Pinch of cayenne pepper
2 tsp/10 g curry powder
1 tsp/5 ml honey
Pinch of turmeric
2 tbsp/30 ml water
2 tbsp/20 g sesame or chickpea
   (garbanzo bean/gram) flour

Makes 2 wraps.

Preheat the oven to 440°F/225°C. Combine the buckwheat flour, psyllium husk fiber, and salt. Whisk in the water and eggs to make a smooth batter and let stand for about 7 minutes. The batter should have a creamy texture. Line a cookie sheet with baking parchment and spread out 2 wraps, each about 10 x 6 inches/25 x 15 cm, using a spatula (dipped occasionally in cold water). Make sure the batter is as evenly distributed as possible and don't leave any holes where the paper shows through. Bake on the middle shelf of the oven for 5–6 minutes and let cool before removing from the paper.

Make sure all the ingredients for the mayonnaise are at room temperature. Whisk up the egg yolk and mustard and then begin to add the oil, drop by drop, whisking vigorously. When you see that it is starting to thicken, add the oil in a steady stream, and whisk until the mayonnaise has the desired consistency. To finish, stir in the lemon juice, lemon zest, honey, and spices to taste. Check the flavor and add more acidity, salinity, heat, or sweetness as required.

Blend all the ingredients for the hummus into a fine and smooth batter. When the wraps have cooled, spread on a layer of hummus then add a little shredded red cabbage, shredded carrot, chopped cherry tomatoes, spinach, parsley, and a dollop of mayonnaise. Roll up the wraps and serve!

Tips If you want to make more wraps, make a new batch of batter while the first is baking instead of doubling the quantity of the batter. The psyllium husk fiber constantly absorbs and locks away liquid the longer it is left to stand, so it can sometimes get a little stodgy if left too long.

VEGETABLE STIR-FRY

with lemon grass & red curry

3 stalks lemon grass
¾ oz/20 g white or red
  cabbage
¾ oz/20 g bell pepper
¼ finely chopped red chili
1 clove of garlic, pressed
1 tsp/1.5 g finely grated
  ginger root
1½ tsp/7.5 ml red curry paste
¼ cup/35 g cooked chickpeas
  (garbanzo beans)
7 tbsp/100 ml full-fat
  coconut milk
Scant ¼ tsp/1.25 g herb salt
¼ tsp/1.25 ml agave syrup
1 tsp/5 ml lime juice
About 2½ oz/70 g Shirataki
  noodles
Coconut oil, for frying

Topping options
Broccoli
Carrot
Sprouts
Fresh cilantro (coriander)

Serves 1.

Finely chop the lemon grass, making sure to trim off the tough stalk at the bottom. Shred the cabbage finely and shred the bell peppers.

Sweat the lemon grass, chili, garlic, ginger, and curry paste in coconut oil in a skillet, then add the white or red cabbage, chickpeas (garbanzo beans), and bell pepper. Pour in the coconut milk and simmer over low heat for about 5 minutes. Add the salt, agave syrup, and lime juice.

Rinse the Shirataki noodles in a colander and place them in a bowl of hot water for 3–4 minutes. Strain the noodles and add them to the wok with the broccoli, carrots, sprouts, and fresh cilantro (coriander) before serving. Squeeze over a little more lime if you like it sharp.

Tips

Shirataki noodles are gluten- and lactose-free and contain practically no carbohydrates. The noodles are almost transparent and are made from glucomannan, which is extracted from konjac root. You can also use rice noodles or egg noodles.

CANDIES
&
DESSERTS

SWEET MUFFINS

with almond & coconut cream

....

Muffins
3½ tbsp/50 g coconut sugar
7 tbsp/50 g coarse almond
  flour
½ cup/50 g finely ground
  coconut flour
½ cup/80 g potato flour
2 tbsp/30 g psyllium husk
  fiber
2 tsp/10 g baking powder
Pinch of salt
3 tbsp/45 ml coconut oil
3 eggs
1¼ tsp/6.25 g finely ground
  cardamom
1 cup/250 ml any milk
Coconut oil, for greasing

6 large or 12 regular-sized
  muffin cups

Almond paste
½ cup/75 g coarse almond
  flour
3 tbsp/45 ml any milk
3 tbsp/45 ml agave syrup

Coconut cream
¾ cup/200 ml coconut cream
1 tsp/5 ml agave syrup
1 tsp/5 ml lemon juice
Pinch of pure vanilla powder

Makes 6 large or 12 small muffins.

Place an ovenproof plate at the bottom of the oven and preheat the oven to 440°F/225°C. Combine all the dry ingredients except the cardamom.

Melt the coconut oil in a saucepan. Whisk up 2 eggs + 1 egg yolk (save the white), the cardamom, and the milk. Whisk the milk mixture into the dry ingredients until you have a smooth, finely textured batter. Let the batter stand for 5 minutes.

Beat the saved egg white to stiff peaks and fold into the batter. Brush the muffin cups with the melted coconut oil, pour in the batter, and place them on a cookie sheet. Place the tray on the middle shelf of the oven, pour 1 tbsp of water onto the heated plate at the bottom, and quickly close the door. Do not open the oven again until the muffins are golden brown. It will take 20–25 minutes for 6 large ones or 12–14 minutes if you make 12 smaller ones. Let the muffins cool on a wire rack.

Mix the ingredients for the almond paste in a bowl, adding a little more liquid if too thick. Whisk the coconut cream ingredients and place the almond paste and coconut cream mixture in the refrigerator.

Cut the tops off the muffins, scoop out a small hole in the middle of each, add a dollop of almond paste, garnish with coconut cream, and replace the lid.

....

Tips
Try to go for muffin cups which are pretty deep so the muffins get a nice shape. Tips for whisking coconut cream can be found under Tips & Techniques on page 11.

CRÈME BRÛLÉE

with coconut milk & blueberries

1⅔ cups/400 ml full-fat
  coconut milk
4 egg yolks
1 egg
3½ tbsp/50 g coconut sugar
  + 4 tsp for sprinkling over
  the top
Generous pinch of pure
  vanilla powder
Generous pinch of coarse
  salt
Blueberries and mint leaves,
  for garnishing

Serves 4.

Preheat the oven to 300°F/150°C.

Whisk all the crème brûlée ingredients together in a bowl. Pour the mixture into 4 ramekins and place them in an ovenproof dish or small roasting pan.

Boil some water and pour it into the dish or pan so that the water comes about halfway up the sides of the ramekins. Bake in the oven for 30–40 minutes for wider, flatter ramekins and 50–60 minutes for taller ramekins. The egg custard should just be thickening but not have gone solid; give it a little shake to check the consistency.

Take out the ramekins and let them cool.

Preheat the oven grill to its hottest setting. Sprinkle 1 tsp coconut sugar onto each crème brûlée, place the ramekin on the top shelf of the oven, and "brown" the sugar; it will burn very quickly, so keep an eye on it at all times. You can also use a blowtorch.

Serve with blueberries and mint.

Tips Crème brûlée tastes amazing with a little grated lemon, orange, or lime zest; cardamom and cinnamon will also give it a real lift. You can get coconut sugar from any well-stocked supermarket, health food store, or online. The ramekins in the picture are the flatter, wider kind.

SAFFRON ICE CREAM

with candied walnuts

Candied walnuts
6 tbsp/40 g walnuts
1 tbsp/15 ml agave or yacon syrup
Pinch of herb salt
Pinch of cayenne pepper

Ice cream
⅔ cup/150 g cashew nut butter
Generous ¾ cup/200 ml almond milk
3½ tbsp/50 ml agave syrup
General pinch of pure vanilla powder
Scant ¼ tsp/1.25 g herb salt
Pinch of saffron
2½ tbsp/37.5 ml melted coconut oil

Serves 2–4.

Place the walnuts in a jar and pour in water to cover the nuts. Let stand for 4 hours in the refrigerator, then pour away the water.

Preheat the oven to 350°F/175°C. Mix the walnuts, syrup, salt, and cayenne pepper in a bowl. Line a cookie sheet with baking parchment, arrange the nuts on top, and roast in the oven for about 20 minutes. Stir the nuts halfway through.

Remove from the oven and let cool.

Combine all ingredients for the ice cream except the coconut oil and whizz with a hand blender or in a food processor until smooth. Melt the coconut oil in a saucepan over low heat and pour into the mixture once it has cooled.

Chop half the walnuts into very small pieces and stir into the ice cream mixture. Save the remaining nuts to garnish the ice cream.

Run the ice cream through an ice cream machine. Alternatively, transfer the mixture into a container with a lid and place in the freezer for 3–4 hours or until it is frozen through. Take out the ice cream 20–30 minutes before serving.

Tips

Candied walnuts are extremely tasty and handy—you can serve them in a salad or eat them as a snack. There are endless possibilities for decorating the ice cream—perhaps some mixed fruit, or why not try chocolate. You can also use another creamy nut or seed butter in the ice cream; pistachio butter is taste heaven!

CHOCOLATE ICE CREAM

with banana & almond butter

....

Ice cream
2 small ripe bananas
1½ tbsp/25 ml milk
1½ tbsp/15 g raw cocoa
1 tsp/5 ml agave syrup
2 tbsp/30 g almond butter
Pinch of coarse salt

Topping
Cocoa nibs
Agave syrup

Serves 1–2.

Peel the bananas and cut into pieces, then place them in the freezer for a few hours until they are completely frozen.

Mix all the ingredients in a food processor or with a hand blender.

Top with a few cocoa nibs and a little agave syrup, and serve immediately.

....

Tips If you like, you can use other nut or seed butters, and you can vary the flavor of the ice cream—mix in a cup of frozen berries and half an avocado, for example, and you'll have a wonderfully creamy berry ice cream.

PEANUT COOKIES

with chocolate

Generous ⅔ cup/100 g
smooth peanut butter
1 egg (room temperature)
1½ tbsp/25 ml coconut oil
(room temperature)
2 tbsp/30 g coconut sugar
1 tbsp/10 g coconut flour
½ tsp/2.5 g baking soda
Pinch of coarse salt
¼ cup/40 g chopped dark
chocolate

Makes 8 cookies.

Preheat the oven to 350°F/175°C.

Mix the peanut butter, eggs, and coconut oil into a paste
in a food processor or with a hand blender. Now mix in
the coconut sugar, then add the coconut flour, baking
powder, and salt, and give it a final mix.

Let the batter rest for a few minutes while you chop the
chocolate. Give the chocolate a quick whizz in the food
processor then finish the chopping by hand and stir the
chocolate into the batter.

Line a cookie sheet with baking parchment and spoon
out 8 equal cookie shapes onto the sheet. Flatten them
down and bake in the oven for 8–10 minutes. Let cool
completely before serving.

You may sometimes find that the coconut oil leaks out
of the batter. If this happens to yours, don't bother trying
to mix the oil back into the mixture; just spoon the
batter onto the cookie sheet, shape the cookies, and leave
the excess oil in the food processor. I have always found
the end results to be amazing either way. Serve with a
glass of iced hazelnut milk! See page 46 for the recipe.

Tips
You could use another creamy nut or seed butter, such as almond, sunflower
seed, hazelnut, or cashew nut butter. Choose a good quality chocolate with at
least 70 percent cocoa content, but without refined sugar or milk.

BERRY PIE

with crunchy buckwheat crumble

....

Berry filling
1¾ cups/175 g thawed
 blueberries
Generous 1 cup/130 g
 thawed raspberries
1 mashed banana
1½ tsp/7.5 g potato flour

Pie topping
1 cup/90 g buckwheat flakes
6 tbsp/60 g buckwheat
 flour
5 tbsp/75 ml coconut oil
Scant ¼ tsp/1.25 g salt
Generous pinch of ground
 cardamom
3½ tbsp/50 ml agave syrup
Coconut oil, for greasing

Coconut cream
¾ cup/200 ml coconut
 cream
1 tsp/5 ml agave syrup
1 tsp/5 ml lemon juice
Pinch of pure vanilla powder

Serves 4–6.

Preheat the oven to 390°F/200°C and grease an 11-inch/28-cm diameter pie dish with some melted coconut oil.

Mix the berries, mashed banana, and potato flour in the pie dish.

Combine the ingredients for the pie topping and press down or sprinkle over the filling.

Bake for 20 minutes on the middle shelf of the oven, or until the pie has turned a golden brown color.

Whisk together the coconut cream ingredients and serve with the pie.

....

Tips

You can also use, for example, amaranth flour and amaranth cereal in the pie. Mixed nuts and seeds also give the pie crumble a delightful flavor and crunch. You'll find some tips for whisking coconut cream under Tips & Techniques on page 11.

BLUEBERRY ROLL

with cinnamon & cardamom

....

Roll
2½ tbsp/37.5 ml coconut oil
   (room temperature)
1½ tbsp/25 ml any milk
Generous pinch of pure
   vanilla powder
1 tsp/5 g ground cinnamon
1 tsp/5 g ground cardamom
2 tbsp/30 g coconut sugar
Generous 1 tbsp/12 g
   coconut flour
Generous 1½ tbsp/12 g
   coarse almond or hazelnut
   flour
1½ tsp/7.5 g baking powder
Pinch of herb salt
2 tbsp/30 g psyllium husk
   fiber
1 egg
2 egg whites

Filling
1 tbsp/15 ml coconut oil
   (room temperature)
1 tsp/5 g ground cinnamon
1 tbsp/15 ml agave syrup
¾ cup/70 g blueberries

Muffin cups

Makes about 10 mini rolls.

Preheat the oven to 390°F/200°C.

Melt the coconut oil in a pan, add the milk, vanilla, cinnamon, cardamom, and coconut sugar, and set aside.

Combine the flour, baking powder, salt, and psyllium husk fiber.

Beat the eggs and egg whites to a foam. Pour in the milk mixture, then add the dry ingredients and mix well. Let the mixture rise for 5–6 minutes.

Roll out the mixture between two sheets of baking parchment to make a layer about 10 x 12 inches/25 x 30 cm. Remove the top sheet. Brush the mixture with coconut oil, sprinkle on some ground cinnamon, drizzle with agave syrup, and scatter over the blueberries.

Roll up the batter from the long side, using the baking parchment to help you. Cut the roll into 10 equal pieces, transfer the pieces to the muffin cups, and bake in the oven for 12–15 minutes.

....

Tips

You can make the rolls with nut or seed flour. If you don't have an almond mill, whizz sunflower seeds, pecans, pistachios, or cashew nuts and the like in a mixer to make a coarse flour. You can also substitute the coconut flour with chickpea flour and sesame flour.

FUDGE

with a hint of lemon

10 pitted dates
⅔ cup/100 g raw cashew
  nuts
3½ tbsp/50 ml melted
  coconut oil
Pinch of pure vanilla powder
Grated zest of 1 lemon
  (washed)
Pinch of herb salt

Makes 15 pieces.

Soak the dates in generous ¾ cup/200 ml of water in a screw-top jar in the refrigerator for 4 hours. At the same time, soak the cashew nuts in 1¼ cups/300 ml of water in a screw-top jar in the refrigerator for 4 hours.

Strain the dates and the cashew nuts, reserving the water from the dates but discarding the water from the cashew nuts.

Melt the coconut oil over low heat, stir in the vanilla, lemon zest, and salt, then whizz up all ingredients in a food processor or with a hand blender.

Line a shallow mold with baking parchment and transfer the mixture to the mold. Place in the freezer for a few hours, then cut into pieces and enjoy!

 Tips
The sweet soaking water left over from the dates is a great ingredient for pastries and smoothies. You can also use sunflower seeds instead of cashews. One hot tip is to add a pinch of saffron to the fudge.

ROCKY ROAD

sweet, salty & spicy

....

5 tbsp/75 ml coconut oil
6 tbsp/55 g raw cocoa
3 tbsp + 1 tsp/50 ml agave syrup
Generous ¾ cup/100 g chopped nuts, e.g. pistachio and walnuts
1 tbsp/15 g nut butter, e.g., hazelnut or pistachio butter
Coarse salt, cayenne pepper, and nuts, for garnishing

Makes approx. 20 pieces.

Melt the coconut oil in a saucepan. Add the remaining ingredients and mix until you have a smooth, finely textured chocolate batter.

Line one large mold or several smaller molds with baking parchment, pour in the batter, and sprinkle a few salt flakes, a little cayenne pepper, and a few nuts on top. Let stand in the refrigerator for a few hours until it has set.

Store the rocky road in the refrigerator until you are ready to cut it into pieces and serve.

....

Tips Use any nuts and seeds you like in the chocolate, and vary the nut butter to taste. Although it tastes good with freeze-dried berries or dried fruit, the chocolate is also delicious when eaten on its own.

CHOCOLATE FUDGE

with chia seeds & hazelnuts

10 pitted dates
4 tbsp/60 ml agave syrup
3 tbsp/30 g chia seeds
5 tbsp/75 ml water, for
  soaking
3 tbsp/45 ml coconut oil
Pinch of pure vanilla powder
Pinch of herb salt
Scant 1 cup/130 g hazelnuts
5–6 tbsp/45–55 g raw cocoa
  + extra for dusting

Makes 20 pieces.

Soak the dates in generous ¾ cup/200 ml of water in a screw-top jar in the refrigerator for 4 hours.

Strain the dates, saving the water. Pour 5 tbsp/75 ml date water over the chia seeds and stir until it forms a thick batter.

Whizz the chia seeds with the remaining ingredients in a food processor or with a hand blender. Taste the batter and add more cocoa or sweetener to taste.

Line a mold with baking parchment and pour in the batter. Once set, store in the refrigerator until you are ready to serve.

To serve, cut into pieces, dust with cocoa, and eat cold.

Tips
Coconut oil is a useful ingredient for baking, roasting, smoothies, oatmeal, and candy. Coconut oil solidifies when it is chilled, but it can be stored at room temperature; it turns into a liquid at approximately 77°F/25°C. Buy a coconut oil that is cold-pressed, raw, and extra virgin. You can also use it as a massage oil, lotion, or as a moisturizing hair treatment.

ENERGY BARS

with chocolate & orange

First layer
Scant 1 cup/130 g raw
  hazelnuts
Generous ¾ cup/120 g
  raisins
Pinch of herb salt
1 tbsp/15 ml water
Pinch of pure vanilla powder

Second layer
⅓ cup/50 g cashews, soaked
  for at least 3 hours and
  drained
7 tbsp/100 ml coconut oil
8 pitted dates
Pinch of herb salt
Pinch of pure vanilla powder

Top layer
5 tbsp/75 ml coconut oil
3½ tbsp/50 ml agave syrup
Grated zest of 1 orange
  (set aside a little for the
  garnish)
5 tbsp/45 g raw cocoa

Makes about 20 bars.

Whizz up the ingredients for the first layer in a food processor or with a hand blender. Line the base of a square baking mold (about 8 x 8 inches/20 x 20 cm) with baking parchment and spread the mixture on top. Place the mold in the freezer.

Reserving the cashew nuts, whizz up the other ingredients for the second layer in a food processor or with a hand blender. Add the nuts and mix to a batter. Spread this on top of the first layer and return the mold to the freezer.

Combine the ingredients for the top layer in a saucepan and heat over low heat until the coconut oil has melted. Pour over the top of the second layer in the mold.

Sprinkle on the reserved orange zest and return the mold to the freezer until the layers have set.

Cut into pieces and serve.

Tips You can use other nuts and seeds in both the first and second layer: almonds, pistachios, sunflower seeds, pumpkin seeds, or pecans, for example.

CHOCOLATE BOMBE

topped with raspberries & pistachios

Cake
Generous ¾ cup/200 ml
  coconut oil
½ cup/110 g coconut sugar
¼ cup/55 g unsweetened
  applesauce
½ tsp/2.5 g pure vanilla
  powder
1 tsp/5 g coarse salt
Generous ½ cup/50 g raw
  cocoa
7 tbsp/100 ml cold strong
  coffee
6 pitted dates
About 3⅓–4 cups/300–360 g
  buckwheat flakes
Coconut oil, for greasing

Chocolate cream
¾ cup/200 ml coconut
  cream
3 tbsp/25 g raw cocoa
½ cup/115 g unsweetened
  applesauce
2 tbsp/30 ml agave syrup
Pinch of coarse salt
Grated zest of ½ lime

Topping
Generous ⅓ cup/30 g
  pistachio nuts
1 cup/100 g raspberries

Serves 10–12.

Melt the coconut oil in a saucepan and mix in the coconut sugar, applesauce, vanilla, salt, cocoa, and coffee until you have a smooth and finely textured batter.

Transfer the chocolate mixture to a food processor, add the dates, and blend; alternatively, if you have a hand blender, you can do this directly in the pan.

Now add the buckwheat flakes a handful at a time and mix by hand or whizz in the food processor until you have a smooth, firm batter. Buckwheat flakes absorb a fair amount of liquid, so don't let the mixture get too dry (or too wet either).

Lightly brush a high-sided springform mold with coconut oil. Use the bottom of a glass jar to press the mixture into the mold, packing it down tightly. Transfer to the refrigerator.

Combine all the ingredients for the chocolate cream. Transfer to the refrigerator. Leave both cake and frosting in the refrigerator for 2–3 hours to set.

Unclip the sides of the springform mold and spread on the chocolate cream, either on the top or all over the cake, as you wish. Top with raspberries and pistachios.

Tips

You can leave out the coffee, but replace it with water so the texture will be right. Don't be fooled by the cake's dainty size, it is very rich and will feed any number of chocolate-starved guests! The idea for the cake actually came from all the times I used to make chocolate truffles when I was little; this is my slightly more grown-up version. A hot tip is also to add a little shredded coconut to the cake.

INDEX

in alphabetical order

INDEX   *arranged by topic*

ACKNOWLEDGMENTS

A big thanks to my amazing family, my wonderful friends, my colleagues, and the whole gang at Max Ström. The support, encouragement, and help I received was invaluable. All the hours in the kitchen achieving the perfect recipe, the time spent editing at the computer, helping out with equipment at photo shoots, the laughter, tears, sweat, and joy would never have been the same without you. You are the best and I'm so glad to have shared this exciting and hectic journey with you.